# Hetherington Surname

# Ireland: 1600s to 1900s

From Ireland Church Records of Baptism, Marriage and Death

Comprised of Roman Catholic and Church of Ireland Records

From Counties Carlow, Cork, Kerry and Dublin City

Compiled by **Donovan Hurst**

March 14, 2012

ISBN: 1939958083
ISBN-13: 978-1-939958-08-2

# Dedication

This work is dedicated to all of those that came before us and shaped
our lives to make us the people that we are today.

# Table of Contents

# Introduction

This is a compilation of individuals who have the surname of Hetherington that lived in the country of Ireland from the 1600s to the 1900s. I have placed each entry into one of four categories: Families, Individual Births/Baptisms, Individual Burials, and Individual Marriages. If a marriage entry primarily concerns an Individual Hetherington whom is female, then I have placed that entry under the category of Individual Marriages. If a marriage entry primarily concerns an Individual Hetherington whom is male, then I have placed that entry under the category of Families. Images of many of these listings are available at http://churchrecords.irishgenealogy.ie/churchrecords/.

To help guide the reader of this work, the format of this book is as follows:

- Main Family Entry (Husband and Wife) (Father and Mother)

  o Child of Main Family Entry, including Spouse(s) when available

    ▪ Grandchild of Main Family Entry, including Spouse(s) when available

      • Great-Grandchild of Main Family Entry, including Spouse(s) when available

(**Bolded Text**) following any entry includes any additional information such as Residence(s), Occupation(s), Signature(s), etc. when available.

# Hurst

Some of the fonts used in this work symbolizes Celtic writing.  The traditional letters, numbers, and punctuation marks and their Celtic counterparts are as follows:

## Traditional Letters (Uppercase & Lowercase)

A a B b C c D d E f G g H h I i J j K k L l M m N n O o P p Q q R r S s T t U u V v W w X x Y y Z z

## Celtic Letters (Uppercase & Lowercase)

A a B b C c D ð E e F f G g H h I i J j K k L l M m

N n O o P p Q q R ʀ S s T t U u V v W w X x Y y Z z

## Traditional Numbers

1 2 3 4 5 6 7 8 9 10

## Celtic Numbers

1 2 3 4 5 6 7 8 9 10

## Traditional Punctuation

. , : ' " & - ( )

## Celtic Punctuation

. , : ' " & - ( )

# Parish Churches

# Carlow (Church of Ireland)

Carlow Parish and Tullow Parish.

# Cork & Ross

# (Roman Catholic or RC)

Cork - SS. Peter & Paul Parish.

# Dublin (Church of Ireland)

Arbour Hill Barracks Parish, Bethseda Chapel Parish, North Strand Parish, Sandford Parish, St. Andrew Parish, St. Audoen Parish, St. Bride Parish, St. Catherine Parish, St. George Parish, St. James Parish, St. John Parish, St. Luke Parish, St. Mark Parish, St. Mary Parish, St. Michan Parish, St. Nicholas Within Parish, St. Nicholas Without Parish, St. Paul Parish, St. Peter Parish, St. Stephen Parish, St. Thomas Parish, and St. Werburgh Parish.

# Dublin (Roman Catholic or RC)

Bohernabreena Parish, Chapelizod Parish, Harrington Street Parish, Rathmines Parish, SS. Michael & John Parish, St. Agatha Parish, St. Andrew Parish, St. Audoen Parish, St. Catherine Parish, St. James Parish, St. Joseph Parish, St. Lawrence Parish, St. Mary, Pro Cathedral Parish, St. Michan Parish, and St. Nicholas Parish.

# Kerry (Roman Catholic or RC)

Dromtariffe Parish and Tralee Parish.

# Families

- Arthur Hetherington & Bridget Hetherington

  o Hugo Hetherington & Martha Mary Doolittle – 7 Oct 1878 (Marriage, **St. Agatha Parish (RC)**)

**Hugo Hetherington (son):**

Residence - Paddington, London - October 7, 1878

**Martha Mary Doolittle, daughter of Thomas Doolittle & Mary Anne Unknown**

**(daughter-in-law):**

Residence - Main Street, Co. Wicklow - October 7, 1878

**Wedding Witnesses:**

**James Doolittle & Mary Hetherington**

- Benjamin Hetherington & Alice Unknown

  o Sarah Hetherington, b. 15 Jun 1841, bapt. 12 Aug 1846 (Baptism, **St. Peter Parish**) & George Cameron – 27 Jul 1869 (Marriage, **St. Peter Parish**)

**Signatures:**

**Sarah Hetherington (daughter):**

Residence - 11 Bishop Street - July 27, 1869

**George Cameron, son of William Cameron (son-in-law):**

Residence - 11 Bishop Street - July 27, 1869

Occupation - Carpenter - July 27, 1869

**William Cameron (father):**

Occupation - Steward

**Benjamin Hetherington (father):**

Occupation - Smith

**Wedding Witnesses:**

**Edward Murphy & Alice Hetherington**

Signatures:

    o   Alice Hetherington – b. 22 Jun 1846, bapt. 12 Aug 1846 (Baptism, **St. Peter Parish**)

Signature:

# Hetherington Surname Ireland: 1600s to 1900s

**Benjamin Hetherington (father):**

  Residence - 22 Whitefriar Street - August 12, 1846

  Occupation - White Smith - August 12, 1846

- Christopher Hetherington & Mary Anne Malone
  - Mary Hetherington & James Delaney – 18 Feb 1884 (Marriage, **Harrington Street Parish (RC)**)

**Mary Hetherington (dauther):**

  Residence - 1st Montague Street - February 18, 1884

**James Delaney, son of Michael Delaney & Margaret Walsh (son-in-law):**

  Residence - 71 South George's Street - February 18, 1884

**Wedding Witnesses:**

**Martin Morris & Teresa Byrne**

- David Hetherington & Margaret Donovan – 13 May 1815 (Marriage, **Cork - SS. Peter & Paul Parish (RC)**)

**Wedding Witnesses:**

**Thomas Donovan, James Haley, & Ellen Donovan**

- David Hetherington & Mary Unknown
  - David Hetherington – bapt. 20 Jul 1736 (Baptism, **St. John Parish**)
- Francis Hetherington & Mary Fitzpatrick
  - Mary Hetherington – bapt. 5 Dec 1842 (Baptism, **St. Nicholas Parish (RC)**)

# Hurst

- George Hetherington & Elizabeth Dawson – 22 Dec 1723 (Marriage, *St. Catherine Parish*)

- George Hetherington & Elizabeth Hetherington

  - George Hetherington – bapt. 17 Oct 1714 (Baptism, *St. Catherine Parish*)

- George Hetherington & Jane Phipps – 2 Nov 1775 (Marriage, *St. Bride Parish*)

*George Hetherington (husband):*

*Occupation - Apothecary - November 2, 1775*

- George Hetherington & Margaret Chamberlain – 27 Nov 1813 (Marriage, *St. Paul Parish*)

  - Margaret Hetherington – bapt. 20 Sep 1819 (Baptism, *St. Paul Parish*)

  - William Augustus Hetherington – bapt. 4 Mar 1836 (Baptism, *St. Paul Parish*)

- George Hetherington & Unknown

  - Lucy Emma Hetherington & Robert Tate – 11 Nov 1873 (Marriage, *St. Stephen Parish*)

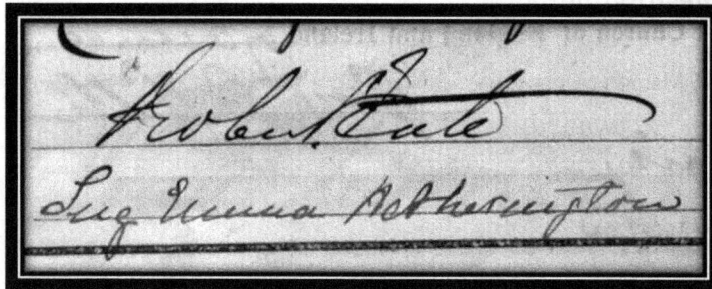

*Signatures:*

*Lucy Emma Hetherington (daughter):*

*Residence - 4 Lower Fitzwilliam Street - November 11, 1873*

*Robert Tate, son of Robert Tate (son-in-law):*

*Residence - Barracks Athlone - November 11, 1873*

*Occupation - Surgeon, 2nd Queen's Regiment*

# Hetherington Surname Ireland: 1600s to 1900s

**Robert Tate (father):**

    Occupation - Gentleman

**George Hetherington (father):**

    Occupation - Medical Doctor

**Wedding Witnesses:**

Charles Edward Hetherington & Richard Tate

**Signatures:**

o    Margaret Anne Hetherington & James Fitzgerald – 8 Apr 1875 (Marriage, **St. George Parish**)

**Signatures:**

**Margaret Anne Hetherington (daughter):**

    Residence - 36 Hardwicke Street - April 8, 1875

# Hurst

James Fitzgerald, son of John Fitzgerald (son-in-law):

    Residence - Hilton Ville, Rathmines - April 8, 1875

    Occupation - Clerk in Holy Orders - April 8, 1875

John Fitzgerald (father):

    Occupation - Esquire

George Hetherington (father):

    Occupation - Medical Doctor

Wedding Witnesses:

Robert Tate & Charles Edward Hetherington

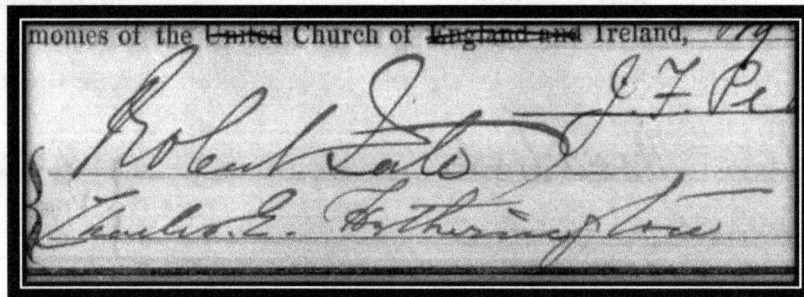

Signatures:

- Gilbert Hetherington & Anne Hetherington
  - James Hetherington – b. 9 Nov 1826, bapt. 19 Nov 1826 (Baptism, **Tullow Parish**)
- Gulielmo Hetherington & Bridget Hyland
  - Mary Helen Hetherington – b. 8 Jul 1876, bapt. 11 Jul 1876 (Baptism, **St. Audoen Parish (RC)**)

Gulielmo Hetherington (father):

    Residence - 10 Lower Bridge Street - July 11, 1876

# Hetherington Surname Ireland: 1600s to 1900s

- Gulielmo Hetherington & Helen Murphy – 26 Feb 1864 (Marriage, **Cork - SS. Peter & Paul Parish (RC)**)

**Gulielmo Hetherington (husband):**

**Residence - 10 Fishamble Lane, Cork - February 26, 1864**

**Helen Murphy (wife):**

**Residence - 10 Fishamble Lane, Cork - February 26, 1864**

**Wedding Witnesses:**

**Thomas Fitzgerald & Catherine McCarthy**

- Hugh Hetherington & Anne Boyle – 13 Jul 1806 (Marriage, **St. Catherine Parish (RC)**)

**Wedding Witnesses:**

**John Parkinson & Mary Anne Cash**

- James Hetherington & Alice Cunningham – 13 Aug 1749 (Marriage, **St. Michan Parish (RC)**)

**Wedding Witnesses:**

**Patrick Lyons, Elizabeth Moore, & Daniel Egly**

- James Hetherington & Lucy Hetherington
  - John Hetherington – bapt. 19 Mar 1782 (Baptism, **Tullow Parish**)
  - William Hetherington – bapt. 18 Feb 1783 (Baptism, **Tullow Parish**)
  - George Hetherington – bapt. 9 Dec 1784 (Baptism, **Tullow Parish**)
  - Sarah Hetherington – bapt. 7 Jan 1788 (Baptism, **Tullow Parish**)
  - Jane Hetherington – bapt. 30 Apr 1790 (Baptism, **Tullow Parish**)

# Hurst

- o James Hetherington – bapt. 29 Feb 1792 (Baptism, **Tullow Parish**)

- o Richard Hetherington – bapt. 29 Feb 1792 (Baptism, **Tullow Parish**)

- o Esther Hetherington – bapt. 13 Jul 1794 (Baptism, **Tullow Parish**)

- o Elizabeth Hetherington – bapt. 20 Nov 1796 (Baptism, **Tullow Parish**)

- o Lucy Hetherington – bapt. 9 Oct 1798 (Baptism, **Tullow Parish**)

- o Gilbert Hetherington – bapt. 16 Feb 1801 (Baptism, **Tullow Parish**)

- James Hetherington & Susan Hetherington

  - o Walter Hetherington – bapt. 9 May 1689 (Baptism, **St. Michan Parish**), bur. 20 Oct 1691 (Burial, **St. Michan Parish**)

  - o Matthew Hetherington – bapt. 10 Apr 1692 (Baptism, **St. Michan Parish**)

## James Hetherington (father):

**Occupation - Glasier - May 9, 1689**

**April 10, 1692**

- John Hetherington & Alice Power – 19 Jul 1840 (Marriage, **St. Andrew Parish** (RC))

  - o Ellen Hetherington & Michael Walsh – 24 Jun 1861 (Marriage, **St. Andrew Parish** (RC))

## Ellen Hetherington (daughter):

**Residence - 31 City Quay - June 24, 1861**

## Michael Walsh, son of Michael Walsh & Sarah Unknown (son-in-law):

**Residence - 19 City Quay - June 24, 1861**

## Wedding Witnesses:

**John Hetherington & Elizabeth Mooney**

- o Patrick Hetherington – bapt. 1845 (Baptism, **St. Andrew Parish (RC)**)

- o Elizabeth Hetherington – b. 1850, bapt. 1850 (Baptism, **St. Andrew Parish (RC)**)

**Wedding Witnesses:**

**Bartholomew Redmond & Margaret Quinn**

- John Hetherington & Anne Unknown

  - o Thomas Hetherington – bapt. 24 Feb 1716 (Baptism, **St. Nicholas Within Parish**)

- John Hetherington & Bridget Darcy

  - o Jane Hetherington – bapt. 21 Oct 1804 (Baptism, **St. James Parish (RC)**)

  - o Michael Hetherington – bapt. 13 Jan 1809 (Baptism, **St. James Parish (RC)**)

- John Hetherington & Eleanor Hetherington

  - o Lucinda Whelan Hetherington – bapt. 18 Jun 1820 (Baptism, **Tullow Parish**)

  - o Jane Hetherington – bapt. 8 May 1821 (Baptism, **Tullow Parish**)

  - o Mary Anne Hetherington – bapt. 24 Nov 1822 (Baptism, **Tullow Parish**)

  - o Amelia Hetherington – bapt. 2 Oct 1825 (Baptism, **Tullow Parish**)

- John Hetherington & Elizabeth MacDermott (M a c D e r m o t t) – 29 Dec 1814 (Marriage, **St. Andrew Parish (RC)**)

**Wedding Witnesses:**

**James Laugtree & Sarah Laugtree**

- John Hetherington & Ellen Hetherington

  - o Eleanor Carter Hetherington – b. 27 Apr 1827, bapt. 27 May 1827 (Baptism, **Tullow Parish**)

  - o Lavina Hetherington – b. 14 Jun 1828, bapt. 13 Jul 1828 (Baptism, **Tullow Parish**)

# Hurst

- John Hetherington & Helen Hetherington
  - Maud Helen Hetherington – b. 21 Sep 1899, bapt. 15 Oct 1899 (Baptism, **Arbour Hill Barracks Parish**)

**John Hetherington (father):**

**Residence - Richmond Barracks, Dublin - October 15, 1899**

**Occupation - Soldier, Corporal A & S Highlanders**

- John Hetherington & Mary MacEntee
  - Mary Hetherington & Edward Sutton – 12 Feb 1899 (Marriage, **St. Mary, Pro Cathedral Parish (RC)**)
    - Bridget Anne Sutton – b. 17 Mar 1900, bapt. 21 Mar 1900 (Baptism, **St. Mary, Pro Cathedral Parish (RC)**)

**Mary Hetherington (daughter):**

**Residence - 27 Upper Dorset Street - February 12, 1899**

**36 upper Dorset Street - March 21, 1900**

**Edward Sutton, son of Patrick Sutton & Bridget Heffernan (son-in-law):**

**Residence - 18 Upper Erne Street - February 12, 1899**

**Wedding Witnesses:**

**Thomas Murray & Bridget Corcoran**

# Hetherington Surname Ireland: 1600s to 1900s

- Joseph Hetherington & Mary Anne Flynn

  o Thomas Cole Hetherington – b. 1899, bapt. 1899 (Baptism, **Chapelizod Parish (RC)**)

**Joseph Hetherington (father):**

**Residence - Chapelizod - 1899**

- Joseph Hetherington & Unknown

  o Joseph Hetherington & Elizabeth Allen – 8 Jun 1876 (Marriage, **St. Michan Parish**)

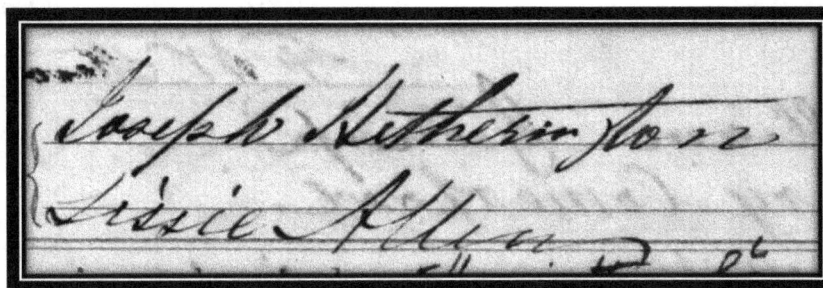

**Signatures:**

**Joseph Hetherington (son):**

**Residence - North Brunswick Street - June 8, 1876**

**Occupation - School Master - June 8, 1876**

**Elizabeth Allen, daughter of John Allen (daughter-in-law):**

**Residence - North Brunswick Street - June 8, 1876**

**John Allen (father):**

**Occupation - Manager in a Drapery Establishment**

**Joseph Hetherington (father):**

**Occupation - Farmer**

# Hurst

**Wedding Witnesses:**

**John Harris & Margaret Harris**

**Signatures:**

- ○ William Hetherington & Mary Jane Wolfe – 28 Apr 1880 (Marriage, **St. George Parish**)

**Signatures:**

- ▪ George Joseph Hetherington – b. 19 Jul 1881, bapt. 25 Sep 1881 (Baptism, **Bethseda Chapel Parish**)

- ▪ Edith Mary Hetherington – b. 17 Oct 1882, bapt. 22 Jan 1883 (Baptism, **Bethseda Chapel Parish**)

- ▪ William Wolfe Hetherington – b. 17 Feb 1884, bapt. 20 Apr 1884 (Baptism, **Bethseda Chapel Parish**)

- ▪ Florence Elizabeth Hetherington – b. 18 Mar 1893, bapt. 28 Sep 1893 (Baptism, **North Strand Parish**)

# Hetherington Surname Ireland: 1600s to 1900s

William Hetherington (son):

    Residence - 84 Phibsborough Road - April 28, 1880

        Laburnum Lodge, Fair View, Richmond - September 25, 1881

                January 22, 1883

        Prospect House, Finglas Bridge - April 20, 1884

        19 Fairview Avenue - September 28, 1893

    Occupation - Merchant - April 28, 1880

        Contractor - September 25, 1881

        April 20, 1884

        Commercial Clerk - January 22, 1883

        Commercial Traveller - September 28, 1893

Mary Jane Wolfe, daughter of George Wolfe (daughter-in-law):

    Residence - 2 botanic View, Glasnevin - April 28, 1880

George Wolfe (father):

    Occupation - Esquire

Joseph Hetherington (father):

    Occupation - Farmer

# Hurst

**Wedding Witnesses:**

George Wolfe & John Hilfirty

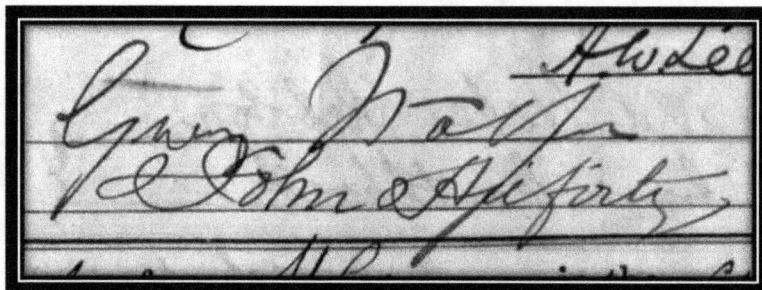

**Signatures:**

- Moses Hetherington & Catherine Hetherington

  o Mary Hetherington – bapt. 15 Jul 1752 (Baptism, **St. Luke Parish**)

- Patrick Hetherington & Elizabeth Mooney

  o Mary Alexandra Hetherington – b. 15 Apr 1868, bapt. 22 Apr 1868 (Baptism, **St. Lawrence Parish (RC)**)

  o John Joseph Hetherington – b. 8 Apr 1870, bapt. 15 Apr 1870 (Baptism, **St. Lawrence Parish** (RC))

**Patrick Hetherington (father):**

Residence - 15 Nixon Street - April 22, 1868

54 Sheriff Street - April 15, 1870

- Patrick Hetherington & Julie Keogh

  o Bridget Mory Hetherington – b. 6 May 1895, bapt. 17 May 1895 (Baptism, **Harrington Street Parish** (RC))

**Patrick Hetherington (father):**

Residence - 6 Montague Street - May 17, 1895

# Hetherington Surname Ireland: 1600s to 1900s

- Robert Hetherington & Ellen Coleman – 5 Oct 1828 (Marriage, **St. George Parish**)

  o Mary Anne Hetherington – b. 10 Aug 1829, bapt. 23 Aug 1829 (Baptism, **St. George Parish**)

  o John Hetherington – b. 1 Mar 1831, bapt. 13 Mar 1831 (Marriage, **St. George Parish**)

  o Irvine Hetherington – b. 29 Apr 1833, bapt. 12 May 1833 (Baptism, **St. George Parish**)

  o Frances Sarah Hetherington – b. 17 Sep 1834, bapt. 5 Oct 1834 (Baptism, **St. George Parish**)

**Robert Hetherington (father):**

**Residence - 33 Great Britain Street - August 23, 1829**

**33 North Great George's Street - March 13, 1831**

**May 12, 1833**

**October 5, 1834**

**Occupation - Servant - August 23, 1829**

**March 13, 1831**

**May 12, 1833**

**October 5, 1834**

- Robert Hetherington & Ellen Unknown

  o Francis Hetherington – b. 22 Jul 1838, bapt. 29 Jul 1838 (Baptism, **St. Peter Parish**)

  o William Hetherington – b. 22 Jul 1838, bapt. 29 Jul 1838 (Baptism, **St. Peter Parish**)

**Robert Hetherington (father):**

**Residence - Leeson Street - July 29, 1838**

# Hurst

- Robert Hetherington & Unknown

  - Elizabeth Hetherington & Thomas Masters – 17 Apr 1855 (Marriage, **St. Mary Parish**)

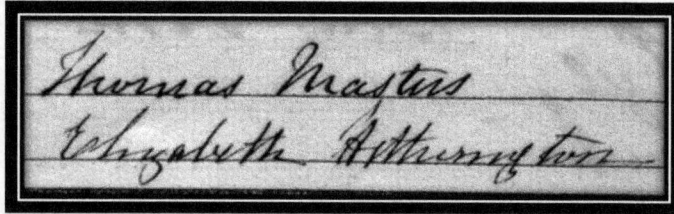

**Signatures:**

**Elizabeth Hetherington (daughter):**

    Residence - 28 Liffey Street - April 17, 1855

**Thomas Masters, son of Charles Masters (son-in-law):**

    Residence - Kilbraecan, Queen's County - April 17, 1855

    Occupation - Farmer - April 17, 1855

**Charles Masters (father):**

    Occupation - Farmer

**Robert Hetherington (father):**

    Residence - Farmer

# Hetherington Surname Ireland: 1600s to 1900s

**Wedding Witnesses:**

**William Walton & Martha Hetherington**

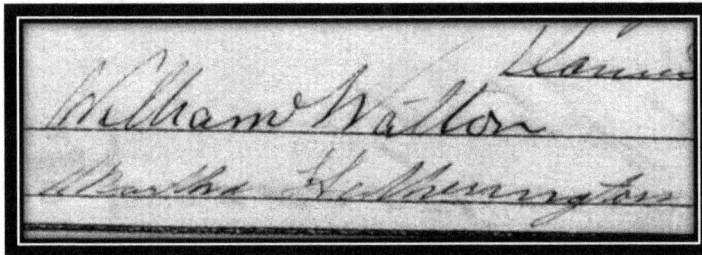

**Signatures:**

- Robert Hetherington & Unknown

  o Robert Hetherington & Jane Collins – 10 Nov 1856 (Marriage, **St. Audoen Parish (RC)**)

**Robert Hetherington (son):**

Residence - 33 Tighe Street - November 10, 1856

**Jane Collins, daughter of Gulielmo Collins (daughter-in-law):**

Residence - 26 Cook Street - November 10, 1856

**Wedding Witnesses:**

**Thomas Stringer & Susan Kilbride**

- Samuel Hetherington & Mary Browne

  o Charles Hetherington – b. 1898, bapt. 1898 (Baptism, **St. Andrew Parish (RC)**)

**Samuel Hetherington (father):**

Residence - Holles Street Hospital - 1898

# Hurst

- Samuel Hetherington & Mary Hetherington

  - Charles Hetherington – b. 10 Nov 1898, bapt. 8 Jan 1899 (Baptism, **St. Mark Parish**)

  - Anne Hetherington – b. 2 Jul 1900, bapt. 11 Jul 1900 (Baptism, **St. Mark Parish**)

**Samuel Hetherington (father):**

**Residence - 36 Deuzille Street - January 8, 1899**

**46 Deuzille Street - July 11, 1900**

**Occupation - Waiter - January 8, 1899**

**July 11, 1900**

- Samuel Hetherington, b. 1773, bur. 28 Dec 1835 (Burial, **St. Werburgh Parish**) & Sarah Hetherington

  - Unknown Hetherington (Male, Child) – bur. 17 Aug 1804 (Burial, **St. Werburgh Parish**)

**Unknown Hetherington (Male, Child) (deceased):**

**Age at Death - 2 weeks**

  - George Hetherington – bapt. 31 Jul 1805 (Baptism, **St. Werburgh Parish**), conf. 5 Jun 1821 (Confirmation, **St. Werburgh Parish**)

  - Elizabeth Hetherington – bapt. 16 Aug 1807 (Baptism, **St. Werburgh Parish**)

  - Susan Hetherington – bapt. 20 Aug 1809 (Baptism, **St. Werburgh Parish**)

  - James Shepard Hetherington, bapt. 11 Aug 1811 (Baptism, **St. Werburgh Parish**), conf. 2 Jun 1827 (Confirmation, **St. Werburgh Parish**) & Mary Hetherington

# Hetherington Surname Ireland: 1600s to 1900s

**Signatures:**

- Leticia Sarah Hetherington – b. 13 Feb 1841, bapt. 14 Mar 1841 (Baptism, **St. Werburgh Parish**)

- Mary Susan Hetherington, b. 5 Apr 1842, bapt. 8 Jun 1842 (Baptism, **St. Werburgh Parish**) &

  Benjamin Thomas Patterson – 11 Jun 1867 (Marriage, **St. Stephen Parish**)

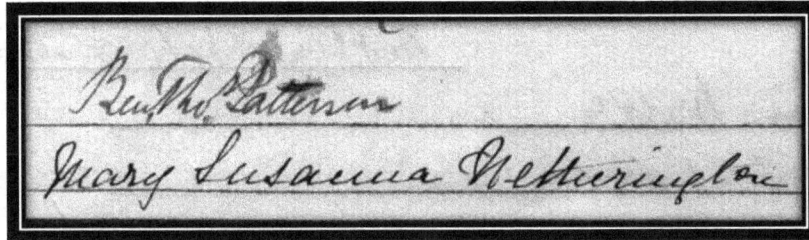

**Signatures:**

**Mary Susanna Hetherington (daughter):**

    Residence - 8 Palmerstown Road, Rathmines - June 11, 1867

**Benjamin Thomas Patterson, son of George Patterson (son-in-law):**

    Residence - Harry Mount Upper Leeson Street - June 11, 1867

    Occupation - Civil Engineer - June 11, 1867

**George Patterson (father):**

    Occupation - Esquire

# Hurst

**James Shepard Hetherington (father):**

Occupation - Esquire

**Wedding Witnesses:**

James Shepard Hetherington & Robert A. Duke

**Signatures:**

- Catherine Hetherington – b. 7 Oct 1843, bapt. 29 Oct 1843 (Baptism, **St. Werburgh Parish**)

- Samuel Hetherington – b. 27 Sep 1845, bapt. 22 Oct 1845 (Baptism, **St. Werburgh Parish**)

- Elizabeth Hetherington – b. 4 Oct 1850, bapt. 4 Dec 1850 (Baptism, **St. Peter Parish**)

- Joseph Hetherington – b. 3 Nov 1859, bapt. 7 Mar 1860 (Baptism, **Sandford Parish**) (Baptism, **St. Peter Parish**)

**James Shepard Hetherington (father):**

Residence - 9 Castle Street - October 29, 1843

October 22, 1845

9 Dunville Avenue, Cullenswood - December 4, 1850

Dunville Avenue - March 7, 1860

Occupation - Merchant - October 29, 1843

October 22, 1845

# Hetherington Surname Ireland: 1600s to 1900s

December 4, 1850

March 7, 1860

o  Mary Hetherington – conf. 27 Jun 1832 (Confirmation, **St. Werburgh Parish**)

o  Sarah Hetherington, conf. 27 Jun 1832 (Confirmation, **St. Werburgh Parish**) & James Barber – 11 Jun 1836 (Marriage, **St. Werburgh Parish**)

Signatures:

James Barber (son-in-law):

Residence - Bishop's Gate, London - June 11, 1836

Wedding Witnesses:

James Shepard & James Shepard Hetherington

Signatures:

Samuel Hetherington (father):

Residence - Castle Street - July 31, 1805

August 16, 1807

August 20, 1809

# Hurst

## August 11, 1811

**Age at Death - 62 years**

- Samuel Hetherington & Unknown

  o Samuel Hetherington & Ellen Brewster Carbin – 18 Oct 1870 (Marriage, **St. Stephen Parish**)

**Signatures:**

  ▪ Samuel Godfrey Hetherington – b. 8 Oct 1872, bapt. 14 Nov 1872 (Baptism, **St. Stephen Parish**)

  ▪ Mary Ellen Olivia Hetherington – b. 7 Feb 1874, bapt. 17 Mar 1874 (Baptism, **St. Peter Parish**)

**Samuel Hetherington (son):**

Residence - 9 Stephen's Lane - October 18, 1870

3 Hender Place - November 14, 1872

3 Walworth Road - March 17, 1874

Occupation - Domestic Servant - October 18, 1870

Butler - November 14, 1872

Servant - March 17, 1874

**Ellen Brewster Carbin, daughter of John Brewster (daughter-in-law):**

Residence - 9 Stephen's Lane - October 18, 1870

Relationship Status at Marriage - widow

**John Brewster (father):**

  Occupation - Land Steward

**Samuel Hetherington (father):**

  Occupation - Famer

**Wedding Witnesses:**

**James Evans & Catherine Evans**

**Signatures:**

- Thomas Hetherington & Bridget Hetherington

  o Abigail Hetherington, b. 17 Feb 1828, bapt. 27 Feb 1828 (Baptism, **St. Luke Parish**) & Richard

     Howell – 15 Jun 1852 (Marriage, **St. Thomas Parish**)

**Signatures:**

**Abigail Hetherington (daughter):**

  Residence - Newcomen Court - June 15, 1852

**Richard Howell, son of William Howell (son-in-law):**

   **Residence - Newcomen Court - June 15, 1852**

   **Occupation - Servant - June 15, 1852**

**William Howell (father):**

   **Occupation - Servant**

**Thomas Hetherington (father):**

   **Occupation - Weaver**

**Wedding Witnesses:**

**George Wills & Frances Wills**

**Signatures:**

- o   Frances Hetherington – b. 17 Nov 1832, bapt. 2 Dec 1832 (Baptism, **St. Luke Parish**)

- o   Elizabeth Hetherington – b. 13 Sep 1835, bapt. 11 Oct 1835 (Baptism, **St. Luke Parish**), bur. 26 Dec 1836 (Burial, **St. Luke Parish**)

**Elizabeth Hetherington (daughter):**

**Residence - Fordam's Alley - Before December 26, 1836**

**Age at Death - 1 ½ years of age**

# Hetherington Surname Ireland: 1600s to 1900s

**Thomas Hetherington (father):**

Residence - Fordam's Alley - February 27, 1828

December 2, 1832

Fordam's Alley No. 13 - October 11, 1835

Occupation - Silk Weaver - February 27, 1828

Silk Engine Weaver - December 2, 1832

Engine Weaver - October 11, 1835

- Thomas Hetherington & Eleanor Unknown
  - o Catherine Hetherington – bur. 26 Jun 1677 (Burial, **St. Audoen Parish**)

- Thomas Hetherington & Margaret Lacy
  - o Michael Hetherington – bapt. 4 Oct 1778 (Baptism, **St. Nicholas Parish** (RC))
  - o Thomas Hetherington – bapt. 14 Apr 1782 (Baptism, **St. Nicholas Parish** (RC))
  - o Nicholas Hetherington – bapt. 7 Dec 1783 (Baptism, **St. Nicholas Parish** (RC))
  - o Francis Hetherington – bapt. 7 Mar 1790 (Baptism, **St. Nicholas Parish** (RC))
  - o Rose Hetherington – bapt. 10 Mar 1791 (Baptism, **St. Nicholas Parish** (RC))

- Timothy Hetherington & Anne Murray
  - o Ellen Hetherington – b. 4 Apr 1895, bapt. 22 Apr 1895 (Baptism, **SS. Michael & John Parish** (RC))
  - o John Hetherington – b. 1896, bapt. 1896 (Baptism, **Bohernabreena Parish** (RC))

**Timothy Hetherington (father):**

Residence - 49 Lower Stephen's Street - April 22, 1895

- Unknown Hetherington & Mary Unknown (1st Marriage)

- Mary Unknown Hetherington (2nd Marriage) & James Williams – 4 Dec 1718 (Marriage, **St. Michan Parish**)

**Mary Unknown Hetherington (wife):**

> **Relationship Status at 2nd Marriage - widow**

**James Williams (husband):**

> **Occupation - Gentleman**

- Unknown Hetherington & Alice Rabiteau – 4 Aug 1759 (Marriage, **St. Nicholas Within Parish**)

**Alice Rabiteau, daughter of John Charles Rabiteau (daughter-in-law).**

- Unknown Hetherington & Jane Collins (1st Marriage)

- Jane Collins Hetherington (2nd Marriage) & Michael Murray – 13 Oct 1873

**Signatures:**

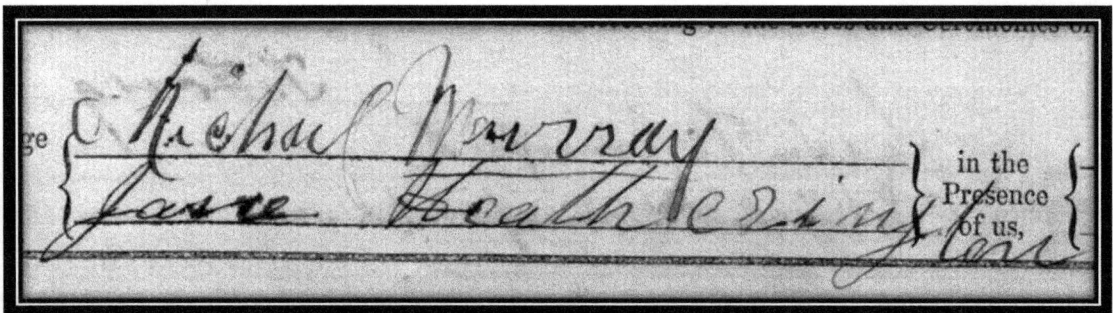

**Jane Collins Hetherington, daughter of William Collins (wife):**

> **Residence - 2 Greek Street - October 13, 1873**

> **Relationship Status at 2nd Marriage - widow**

**Michael Murray, son of William Murray (son-in-law):**

Residence - Meath Hospital - October 13, 1873

Occupation - Servant - October 13, 1873

**William Murray (father):**

Occupation - Blacksmith

**William Collins (father):**

Occupation - Silk Weaver

**Wedding Witnesses:**

Joseph McDee & Emily Smith

**Signatures:**

- William Hetherington & Amistis Unknown
  - William Hetherington – b. 1767, bapt. 21 Apr 1767 (Baptism, **St. Catherine Parish (RC)**)
- William Hetherington & Anne McConnick – 18 Feb 1798 (Marriage, **St. Mary Parish**)
- William Hetherington & Anne Tench
  - Ellen Hetherington – b. 1868, bapt. 1868 (Baptism, **St. Andrew Parish (RC)**)

**William Hetherington (father):**

Residence - 27 Exchequer Street - 1868

# Hurst

- William Hetherington & Anne Unknown

  - John Hetherington – b. 15 Jun 1805, bapt. 24 Jun 1805 (Baptism, **St. Nicholas Within Parish**)

  - Anne Hetherington – b. 17 Dec 1807, bapt. 27 Dec 1807 (Baptism, **St. Nicholas Within Parish**)

- William Hetherington & Christine Young

  - Gulielmo Hetherington – b. 31 May 1912, bapt. 5 Jun 1912 (Baptism, **St. Joseph Parish (RC)**)

**William Hetherington (father):**

**Residence - White Hall, Templeogue - June 5, 1912**

- William Hetherington & Eleanor Hozier – 11 Dec 1814 (Marriage, **St. Andrew Parish**)

- William Hetherington & Elizabeth Hetherington

  - George Hetherington – bapt. 20 Jan 1743 (Baptism, **St. Mary Parish**)

- William Hetherington & Elizabeth Unknown

  - Elizabeth Hetherington – bapt. 28 Sep 1737 (Baptism, **St. John Parish**)

- William Hetherington & Ellen Foley

  - Anne Hetherington – b. 24 Nov 1830, bapt. 24 Nov 1830 (Baptism, **Tralee Parish (RC)**)

**William Hetherington (father):**

**Residence - Tralee - November 24, 1830**

- William Hetherington & Ellen Murphy

  - William Hetherington – b. 18 Sep 1868, bapt. 27 Sep 1868 (Baptism, **Cork - SS. Peter & Paul Parish (RC)**)

  - John Hetherington – b. 11 Jan 1871, bapt. 22 Jan 1871 (Baptism, **Cork - SS. Peter & Paul Parish (RC)**)

28

# Hetherington Surname Ireland: 1600s to 1900s

- o Mary Anne Hetherington – b. 19 Jan 1874, bapt. 25 Feb 1874 (Baptism, **Cork - SS. Peter & Paul Parish (RC)**)

- o James Hetherington – b. 16 May 1877, bapt. 28 May 1877 (Baptism, **Cork - SS. Peter & Paul Parish (RC)**)

- o Christine Hetherington – b. 5 Jan 1880, bapt. 22 Jan 1880 (Baptism, **Cork - SS. Peter & Paul Parish (RC)**)

- William Hetherington & Ellen Unknown
  - o William Hetherington & Roseanne Finnegan – 17 Apr 1882 (Marriage, **St. Michan Parish (RC)**)

**William Hetherington (son):**

Residence - Cumlin - April 17, 1882

**Roseanne Finnegan, daughter of Bernard Finnegan & Roseanne Unknown**

**(daughter-in-law):**

Residence - 2 Henrietta Place - April 17, 1882

**Wedding Witnesses:**

**James Finnegan & Bridget Hoolahan**

- William Hetherington & Mary Unknown
  - o Mary Hetherington – bapt. 16 Apr 1739 (Baptism, **St. John Parish**)
- William Hetherington & Mary Unknown
  - o William Hetherington – bapt. 29 Sep 1782 (Baptism, **St. Catherine Parish**)

**William Hetherington (father):**

Residence - Cork Street - September 29, 1782

# Individual Baptisms/Births

- Elizabeth Hetherington – bapt. 5 Aug 1739 (Baptism, **St. Paul Parish**)

# Individual Burials

- Abigail Hetherington – b. 1763, bur. 7 Jan 1827 (Burial, **St. Luke Parish**)

- Abigail Hetherington – b. 1780, bur. 17 Jan 1848 (Burial, **Carlow Parish**)

**Abigail Hetherington (deceased):**

Residence - Carlow - before January 17, 1848

- Anne Hetherington – b. 1743, bur. 26 Jul 1816 (Burial, **St. Catherine Parish**)

**Anne Hetherington (deceased):**

Residence - Leinster Street - before July 26, 1816

- Catherine Hetherington – bur. Aug 1712 (Burial, **St. Nicholas Without Parish**)

**Catherine Hetherington (deceased):**

Residence - New Row - before August 1712

- David Hetherington – bur. 11 Feb 1741 (Burial, **St. Catherine Parish**)

**David Hetherington (deceased):**

Age at Death - child

- Elizabeth Hetherington – b. 1821, bur. 5 Jul 1824 (Burial, **St. Catherine Parish**)

**Elizabeth Hetherington (deceased):**

Residence - Elbow Lane - before July 5, 1824

# Hurst

- Frances Hetherington – bur. 11 Feb 1767 (Burial, **St. Audoen Parish**)

**Frances Hetherington (deceased):**

**Residence - Corn Market - before February 11, 1767**

- George Hetherington – bur. 7 Jan 1714 (Burial, **St. Catherine Parish**)

- Jane Hetherington – b. 1828, bur. 19 Sep 1838 (Burial, **St. Luke Parish**)

**Jane Hetherington (deceased):**

**Residence - Fordam's Alley - before September 19, 1838**

**Age at Death - 10 years of age**

- John Hetherington – bur. 25 May 1712 (Burial, **St. Nicholas Without Parish**)

**John Hetherington (deceased):**

**Residence - Mill Street - before May 25, 1712**

- John Hetherington – b. 1807, bur. 2 Jul 1816 (Burial, **St. Catherine Parish**)

**John Hetherington (deceased):**

**Residence - Ross Lane - before July 2, 1816**

- Joseph Hetherington – b. 1798, bur. 21 Aug 1832 (Burial, **St. Peter Parish**)

**Joseph Hetherington (deceased):**

**Residence - Portobello Barracks - before August 21, 1832**

**Age at Death - 34 years of age**

# Hetherington Surname Ireland: 1600s to 1900s

- Margaret Hetherington – bur. 11 Oct 1819 (Burial, **St. James Parish**)

**Margaret Hetherington (deceased):**

    **Residence - Barrack Street - before October 11, 1819**

- Mary Hetherington (Child) – bur. 15 Jan 1726 (Burial, **St. Catherine Parish**)
- Prudentia Hetherington – b. 1785, bur. 9 Aug 1831 (Burial, **St. Mark Parish**)

**Prudentia Hetherington (deceased):**

    **Residence - William Street - before August 9, 1831**

    **Age at Death - 46 years of age**

- Richard Hetherington – bur. 5 Apr 1770 (Burial, **St. Paul Parish**)

**Richard Hetherington (deceased):**

    **Residence - Ballybough Bridge - before April 5, 1770**

- Thomas Hetherington – bur. 2 Nov 1689 (Burial, **St. Catherine Parish**)
- Thomas Hetherington – b. 1756, bur. 21 Oct 1826 (Burial, **St. Catherine Parish**)

**Thomas Hetherington (deceased):**

    **Residence - Earl Street - before October 21, 1826**

- Thomas Hetherington – b. 1775, bur. 30 Sep 1830 (Burial, **St. Mark Parish**)

**Thomas Hetherington (deceased):**

    **Residence - Malabride - before September 30, 1830**

    **Age at Death - 55 years of age**

# Hurst

- Unknown Hetherington – bur. 11 Nov 1810 (Burial, **St. John Parish**)

- Unknown Hetherington (Mrs.) – bur. 16 Dec 1828 (Burial, **Carlow Parish**)

# Individual Marriages

- Anne Hetherington & John Howard

  - Sarah Howard – bapt. 12 Jun 1791 (Baptism, **St. Catherine Parish** (RC))

- Catherine Hetherington & John Curtin

  - Thomas Curtin – bapt. 3 Nov 1840 (Baptism, **Cork - SS. Peter & Paul Parish** (RC))

- Eleanor Hetherington & James Robinson – 28 Nov 1813 (Marriage, **St. James Parish**)

- Eleanor Hetherington & Thomas Byrne (B y r n e)

  - Mary Anne Byrne (B y r n e) – bapt. 28 Jan 1782 (Baptism, **St. Catherine Parish** (RC))

  - Richard Joseph Byrne (B y r n e) – bapt. 12 Apr 1784 (Baptism, **St. Catherine Parish** (RC))

  - Peter Byrne (B y r n e) – bapt. 17 Dec 1786 (Baptism, **St. Catherine Parish** (RC))

  - Elizabeth Byrne (B y r n e) – bapt. 15 Feb 1789 (Baptism, **St. Catherine Parish** (RC))

  - John Byrne (B y r n e) – bapt. 4 Mar 1792 (Baptism, **St. Catherine Parish** (RC))

- Elizabeth Hetherington & Adam Fleming – Unknown (Marriage, **St. Werburgh Parish**)

- Elizabeth Hetherington & Michael Lynch

  - Michael Lynch – b. 6 Nov 1881, bapt. 6 Nov 1881 (Baptism, **Dromtariffe Parish** (RC))

  - John Lynch – b. 19 Oct 1885, bapt. 22 Oct 1885 (Baptism, **Dromtariffe Parish** (RC))

  - Daniel Lynch – b. 4 Feb 1890, bapt. 6 Feb 1890 (Baptism, **Dromtariffe Parish** (RC))

**Michael Lynch (father):**

**Residence - Carraraig - November 6, 1881**

**October 22, 1885**

**February 6, 1890**

35

# Hurst

- Elizabeth Hetherington & Robert Giltrap – 9 Nov 1823 (Marriage, **Tullow Parish**)

- Ellen Hetherington & John Baird

  o Robert Christopher Baird – b. 1895, bapt. 1895 (Baptism, **St. Andrew Parish** (RC))

**John Baird (father):**

**Residence - 8 Upper Mercer Street - 1895**

- Jane Hetherington & William Thomlinson – 19 Feb 1811 (Marriage, **Tullow Parish**)

- Lucinda Hetherington & James Hughes – 13 Feb 1821 (Marriage, **Tullow Parish**)

- Louise Hetherington & Patrick Fagan

  o William Fagan – b. 7 Aug 1889, bapt. 12 Aug 1889 (Baptism, **SS. Michael & John Parish** (RC))

  o Mary Josephine Fagan – b. 6 Mar 1891, bapt. 9 Mar 1891 (Baptism, **SS. Michael & John Parish** (RC))

  o Margaret Josephine Fagan – b. 3 Jul 1894, bapt. 9 Jul 1894 (Baptism, **SS. Michael & John Parish** (RC))

  o Louise Fagan – b. 14 Feb 1896, bapt. 17 Feb 1896 (Baptism, **SS. Michael & John Parish** (RC))

  o Ellen Fagan – b. 16 Jan 1898, bapt. 20 Jan 1898 (Baptism, **SS. Michael & John Parish** (RC))

**Patrick Fagan (father):**

**Residence - 2 Cuffe Street - August 12, 1889**

**March 9, 1891**

**July 9, 1894**

**February 17, 1896**

**January 20, 1898**

# Hetherington Surname Ireland: 1600s to 1900s

- Mary Hetherington & John Barry

  o Margaret Barry – bapt. Dec 1818 (Baptism, **St. Michan Parish (RC)**)

- Mary Hetherington & John Nowlan

  o Elizabeth Nowlan – bapt. 4 May 1849 (Baptism, **St. Michan Parish (RC)**)

- Mary Hetherington & Patrick Connor

  o Catherine Connor & Joseph McClean – 10 Jun 1895 (Marriage, **Rathmines Parish (RC)**)

**Catherine Connor (daughter):**

**Residence - 5 Metcalfe Terrace - June 10, 1895**

**Joseph McClean, son of Christopher McClean & Teresa O'Toole (son-in-law):**

**Residence - 11 Shamrock Villa - June 10, 1895**

**Wedding Witnesses:**

**John Curtis & Mary McClean**

- Patricia Hetherington & Timothy Sullivan

  o Timothy Sullivan – b. 5 May 1833, bapt. 5 May 1833 (Baptism, **Dromtariffe Parish (RC)**)

**Timothy Sullivan (father):**

**Residence - Coolclogh - May 5, 1833**

- Sarah Hetherington & Joseph Gilbert – 6 May 1809 (Marriage, **Tullow Parish**)

# Name Variations

Includes Latin and Abbreviated forms of names found in the original documents.

Abigail = Abigale, Abigall

Anne = Ann, Anna, Annae

Bartholomew = Barth, Bartholmeus, Bartholomeo

Bridget = Birgis, Brigid, Brigida, Bridgit

Catherine = Catharine, Catharina, Catharinae, Catherina, Cath, Catha, Cathae, Cathe, Cathn, Kate

Charles = Carolus, Charls, Chas

Christopher = Christoph

Daniel = Danielem, Danielis

Edmund = Edmond

Edward = Ed, Edwd

Eleanor = Eleo, Eleonora, Elinor, Ellenor

Elizabeth = Betty, Elisa, Elisabeth, Eliz, Eliza, Elizab, Elizh, Elizth

Ellen = Elena, Ellena

Emily = Emilia

Esther = Essie, Ester

Francis = Fransicum

George = Geo, Georg, Georgius

Grace = Gratiae

Gulielmo = Guil, Guillelmi, Gulielmum, Guillelmus, Gulmi

Helen = Helena

# Hetherington Surname Ireland: 1600s to 1900s

Honor = Hanora, Honora

James = Jacobi, Jacobus, Jas

Jane = Joanna

Jeanne = Jeannae, Joannae

Joan = Johanna, Joney

John = Jno, Joannem, Joannes, Johannis

Joseph = Jos

Juliana = Julian

Leticia = Letitia, Lettice, Letticia

Lewis = Louis

Luke = Lucas

Margaret = Margarita, Margaritae, Margeret, Marget, Margt

Martha = Marthae

Mary = Maria, My

Mary Anne = Marianna, Marianne, Maryanne

Michael = Michaelis, Michl

Patrick = Pat, Patt, Patk, Patricii, Patricius

Peter = Petri

Richard = Ricardi, Ricardus, Rich, Richd

Robert = Roberti

Rose = Rosa, Rosae

Thomas = Thom, Thomae, Thoms, Thos, Ths

Timothy = Timotheus, Timy

William = Wil, Will, Willm, Wm

# Notes

# Notes

# Notes

# Notes

# Notes

# Notes

# Index

# Hurst

# Hetherington Surname Ireland: 1600s to 1900s

## W

# About The Author

Donovan Hurst graduated from San Diego State University with a Bachelor of Arts in the major field of studies of History and a minor in the field of studies of Anthropology. He is a current member of The General Society of Mayflower Descendants and has been conducting genealogical research for over 10 years tracing back his ancestors to their ancestral homelands in Denmark, England, France, Germany, Ireland, Norway, and Scotland.

www.ingramcontent.com/pod-product-compliance
Lightning Source LLC
Chambersburg PA
CBHW081201270326
41930CB00014B/3254